STRIKING CLOSE TO HOME

Other Books by John McPherson

Adventures of Buck Felner
Close to Home Unplugged
Home: The Final Frontier
The Honeymoon Is Over
McPherson Goes to Church
McPherson's Marriage Album
One Step Closer to Home
The Silence of the Lamberts

STRIKING CLOSE TO HOME

A CLOSE TO HOME Collection by John McPherson

ZondervanPublishingHouse

Grand Rapids, Michigan

A Division of HarperCollins*Publishers*

Special thanks to Peggy McKeehan for her wonderful
watercolor work on the cover of this book.

Thanks also to Chris Millis for his graphic assistance and overall moral support.

"This is what I get for marrying a crossword puzzle fanatic."

"For crying out loud! Can't you take a hint?!
Get outside and play ball with your son!"

"I hope you don't already have one of these!"

On days when the weather was really lousy,
Dorothy relied on her radio-controlled dog walker.

"Take one of these precisely every 10,187 seconds and exactly 37 seconds after eating a bologna and cucumber sandwich on rye bread. 112 seconds later, drink 3.78 ounces of buttermilk and eat 3 1/2 green M&M's."

"Ray? No! Believe it or not, Jason caught it using a toy fishing pole and a piece of Play-Doh as bait!"

"Our metal detector is broken. Please lie flat on the conveyor with your luggage in front of you."

After treating his patients, Dr. Wainsmith loved to watch the expression on their faces when they looked in the funhouse mirror he had mounted on his wall.

The Transit Authority makes a desperate attempt to promote a friendlier atmosphere by hiring hospitality hostesses.

"As a $700 option, we can install a windshield that's customized to match your glasses prescription."

Bob was beginning to sense some negative body language from his interviewer.

"The only way we can keep the baby from crying is if we hold her at a forty-five degree angle while hopping clockwise on one foot."

"It wasn't nearly as serious as we first thought. He needed only two stitches."

"They no longer make replacement mufflers for your car. The best I can do is sell you these earphones for $35."

"Get rid of them?! On the contrary, Mr. Westford. Because the geese have begun to nest here, your pool has been declared a protected wetland, requiring that no human activity take place within 150 feet."

Although Eric appreciated the ride, he felt a certain uneasiness the entire time he was in the car.

Shortly after Bryan was knocked unconscious, management put an end to lunch-hour chicken fights.

After repeated complaints from neighbors about Nipper's barking, the Vertmans finally relented and got a dog silencer.

Standard procedure after taking sick leave at Maxwell Global Industries.

"I'm afraid you've got terminal dandruff."

"Calm down, Mrs. Nursteen. There's nothing to be alarmed about. This is just some protective gear to shield us from any bits and pieces that might happen to be whizzing around the room during your root canal."

Seven minutes away from the most important presentation of his career, Ed Lipkin forgets his computer password.

Missing simple putts automatically triggered the course's laugh track system.

The hazards of call waiting: Though she thought she was talking to her grandson, Carol was actually talking to her boss.

To discourage office romances, employees at Mickford Industries were required to eat a clove of garlic each morning.

Unbeknownst to Patty, Scott had registered them for wedding gifts at The Sportsman's Superstore.

"It's all right, Bill! Let him drive the car into the garage! We won a week of free valet parking in a contest on the radio!"

24

"Ever since the last of the kids went off to college, Helen has had a serious case of empty-nest syndrome."

"Hey, that was great, Billy! Well, how about it? Do we have any other children who would like to fly the plane for a while?"

"Congratulations! You're going to have a disease named after you!"

Eckley Industries takes a fresh approach to layoffs.

At last, help for people who hate
to write thank-you notes.

"It's all right. I wrote our **PIN** number
underneath this counter last year."

"I just figured, 'Hey, life's too short to waste any of it cleaning the house,' so I had Bert install an automatic cleaning system."

"For cryin' out loud! What the heck kind of
health insurance do you have anyway?"

"When I slow down, the music on the radio slows down. When I speed up, it sounds like I'm listening to Alvin and the Chipmunks."

Daryl's new hand enhancer dramatically improved his chances of being called on in class.

"Here it is, 144 Ingersoll Road. It's got a one-star rating. In '97 they gave out celery, no one was home in '96, and in '95, their dog bit a kid on the head and ate all his candy."

Maternity nurse Celia Cratchner devises an ingenious money-making scheme.

From humble beginnings, Ernie turns a foul-up at the food-processing plant into a 2,000-restaurant fast-food chain.

"You've always got to try to find a shortcut, don't you?!"

After twelve years of being totally ignored during her safety presentations, flight attendant Velma Forb finally lost it.

"Who's the wiseguy down in X-ray?"

Fortunately, Ken was wearing his
artificial tear-away legs.

"I hope you don't mind, Ron, but I took the liberty of writing up a report card on our date last night."

"After the oral surgeon took out the fourth wisdom tooth, he discovered there were four *more!* Can you believe it?! Eight wisdom teeth, all removed at one time!"

With the due date just days away, and still clueless about what to name their baby, the Lorfners finally called 1-900-KIDNAME.

"It's all part of Dr. Schlemmer's dedication to streamlining his dental service. Hole four, please, Mrs. Maxwell."

The invention of the fax machine has taken some of the charm out of passing notes in class.

After failing to get the waiter's attention using conventional means, Bruce brought out the flare.

"Go down this hallway. Take the fourth left, then the third right. Go down a long corridor, up two flights of stairs, and you'll see a large sign that says Wembley Chiropractic Associates."

When car alarms start to fail.

**"Here's another very popular snout. This one
conveys an air of simple elegance that says
'I'm a sophisticated dog of the '90s.'"**

After having to wear hideous bridesmaid's outfits at the
weddings of her two closest friends, Donna welcomed
the opportunity to carry out her revenge.

As the surgical team entered, Cheryl's confidence in her balloon angioplasty procedure quickly faded.

44

At last, help for chronic oversleepers.

The Weeblers' tenth anniversary dinner is ruined when they catch a fleeting glimpse of what looked like their baby sitter driving by in their newly restored '66 Corvette.

How teachers prepare for an upcoming school vacation.

"Would you like to have regular or our new cherry-flavored Novocain?"

"Not a single mammal was killed to make this coat. It's made entirely out of woolly caterpillars."

Following a tip from an anonymous informant, two ushers uncover the largest popcorn-smuggling operation in the history of U.S. movie theaters.

"I'm sorry, ma'am, but the mall is at maximum capacity.
You'll have to wait until someone leaves."

An amateur magician as well as an obstetrician, Dr. Kingsley felt it was important to bring some humor into the delivery room.

Police in Wagmon County devise an effective method for pulling over speeders.

"She's not supposed to be in school today. All of the kids telecommute on Thursdays and Fridays."

The agony of having a college roommate
with an easy course load.

As a special service, Dr. Gremley gave all of
his patients a complimentary photo-collage
of their entire root-canal procedure.

Although common sense told Bernice to leave the button alone, morbid curiosity drove her to press it.

"Our anesthesiologist is out with a head cold. When I say 'now,' bite on this stick as hard as you can."

"We could save ourselves a lot of time and energy if you'll just follow me over to that toy store and get me the stuff I want right now."

No one ever messed with Wayne's car security
system, crude though it was.

"With the kids tromping in and out in
this messy weather, the electric doormat
has been a godsend."

"The main difference is that that system will be obsolete in eight months, whereas, for only $400 more, you can have a system that's guaranteed not to be obsolete for a full year."

"We don't know what those things are, but everyone who has bought one says they're very affectionate."

To help its customers make those tough gift decisions,
Wagler's Department Store devised Compute-a-Gift.

"I'm sorry, sir, but there's a five-day waiting period on all in-line skate purchases so we can verify that you're not a spaz."

"The intern who worked on me was an art major before going to med school."

"Those are the new relaxed fit jeans."

"To discourage anybody from shaking the gifts, one of those boxes has been filled with hornets. Yep, I hate to think what those hornets might do if anybody shook their box."

"I'm getting sick and tired of cleaning your hair out of the tub! From now on when you shower, I want you to wear this hair strainer around your neck."

"Once the needle platform senses a weight of approximately twenty fallen needles, an electric signal is sent to the microprocessor, which in turn tells that electric valve exactly how much water the tree requires."

"To ensure that your artificial heart functions properly, it's essential that you change your oil and filter every 100 miles."

"I'm afraid it's a bit more involved than we thought. There's a bed in the back room along with some pajamas and a toothbrush."

"Your doctor appears to have written your prescription in some form of ancient Sanskrit. We've got our team of linguists working on it and are hoping to decipher it within forty-eight hours."

"We'll be back with more of your favorite holiday melodies after this brief word from our sponsor."

"I had T-shirts made up with the baby's ultrasound on them!
I thought you could wear yours to your basketball league!"

"Well, don't just stand there, silly! Go and try it out!"

"Oh, shoot! Donna, could you run up to supply on the eighth floor and get me some correction tape?"

The new secretary was starting to get on Doug's nerves.

More and more car buyers are opting
for driver's side periscopes.

"You don't pay any points for this mortgage.
You will, however, be required to baby-sit the
bank manager's kids every Saturday night
for the first five years of the loan."

"For an additional $25, we can airbrush your photo to get rid of that mole and most of those blotchy age spots."

"Mommy's having quiet time now, honey.
Go play with the other kids in the family room."

"I'll give you a thirty percent discount if you'll drop my mother off in Toledo on your way to Des Moines."

"Ya know, you're not exactly doing wonders for morale around here."

"Ma'am, I distinctly saw you turn completely around in your seat to give that child his pacifier. I'm afraid I'm going to have to charge you with driving under the influence of toddlers."

"This unit has a built-in scale so you can just keep working out until you hit your target weight."

"Isn't that sweet?! It's the kids' way of saying they don't want you to go away on your business trip!"

"Be careful. This plate is very hot."

Wayne's faith in his new **HMO** was
eroding quickly.

"You are *both* tremendously talented applicants
and we simply couldn't decide who should
get the division chief position, so . . ."

"It says we can't make any withdrawals today
until we explain how we blew the hundred bucks
we took out yesterday."

"We had your prescription made into a necklace
so you won't forget to take your pills."

"It's a card about the Wilcox-Heffelman wedding.
We're not invited, but we're ninth on the standby
list in case they get any cancellations."

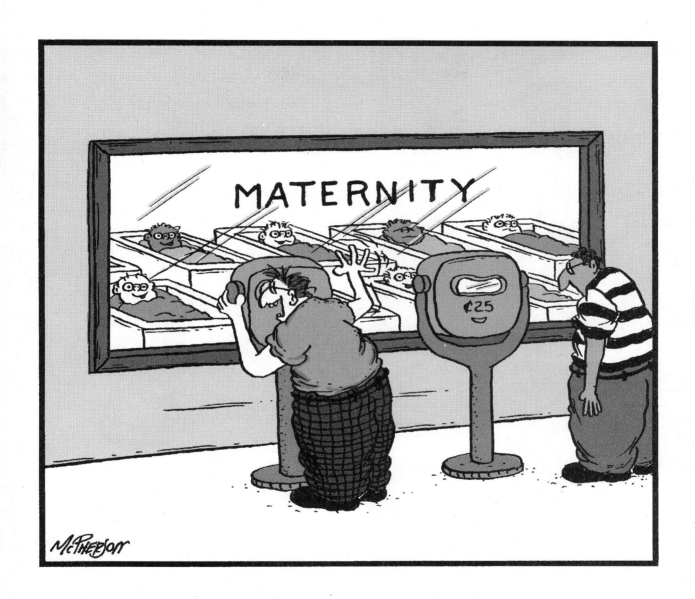

"Hey, if you hit three deer in five weeks you'd start to take some precautions, too."

Ramona Kelpman succumbs to post-holiday apathy.

"Thank heavens you were able to find it!
Now all you need to do is hook it back up!"

Thanks to some virtually invisible fishing line, Nurse Kretchner was able to evoke some priceless facial expressions from proud parents and grandparents.

"Here's twenty bucks. Let 'em keep riding until we get out of the movies."

"Gene, e-mail the kids and tell them
to come downstairs for dinner."

"Wade here thinks it's your distributor. I think it's definitely your carburetor. So we're gonna compromise and replace your water pump."

"We'll take fifty percent off your bill if you'll agree to wear this shirt every Wednesday for a year."

Fewer and fewer plumbers are making housecalls.

Carol had the foresight to record Ed's comments before he started the project.

"Dr. Vernley prides himself on his commitment to 100 percent organic dentistry. Today he'll be using bamboo drill bits, a yucca extract painkiller, and adobe fillings."

"Congratulations, sir! You're the state's one-millionth speeder!"

Flegner Industries adopts a new applicant-screening process.

Closing time at Adventure Zone Playland.

Tired of constantly searching for the TV remote, Sven opts for one of the new remote implants.

Fortunately, Dave had a can of
Cop-Be-Nice in the car.

"To help distract you during your gum surgery,
Ms. Parker will be performing one of
her engaging puppet shows."

Gradually, employees at Milnard Industries
began to abuse the company's
Friday casual-dress policy.

As soon as the Fernquists spotted the house's built-
in piano, Carl knew the sale was in the bag.

"Nurse Wright, when I give the signal, you slap that Band-Aid on him as fast as possible."

"It took some getting used to, but the kids love it.
Plus, I don't have to vacuum anymore."

Unfortunately, Brad had neglected to stretch his brain before taking the big algebra midterm.

"Are you sure? Studies have shown that holding and caressing animals can dramatically speed a person's recovery!"

Common parenting nightmares.

"You can take our standard retirement package, or you can trade it for what Carol has behind door No. 2."

More and more wedding parties are opting for Silly String over rice.

"They must've announced it three times! 'At this time, we ask that passengers please turn off all electronic equipment.' Did you listen?! *No!* You just kept banging away on your stupid laptop!"

How personnel managers actually make their hiring decisions.

In a technological breakthrough that revolutionized the space industry, NASA successfully launches the first space shuttle mission to be activated by The Clapper®.

"Your new pacemaker operates on the same principle as a bumper car at an amusement park."

The Girl Scouts expand their operation.

Knowing the Ridleys' habit of departing hastily whenever he started to show a home video, Duane secretly disconnected their car's ignition coil.

"OK, hold perfectly still! We go with whatever name the baby kicks at!"

"There! Maybe *now* you three will remember to take your plates to the kitchen after dinner!"

Surgeons at Wilton Medical Center prepare
for the world's first beer-bellyectomy.

Inspired by a children's book he had seen, Todd
incorporated sound buttons into his resume.

"It's called 'Sounds of the Dentist's Office.' Dr. Millis
recommends we play it for an hour every day to
encourage all of us to brush and floss."

**Midway through Dave's oral report,
Mrs. Rosemont realizes that he's been lip-syncing.**

**The SPCA quickly cracked down on
Ray's driveway-shoveling scheme.**

As the rash of lunchbag break-ins escalated, many employees in the office began to use The Lunch Club® to safeguard their food.

Krepner Industries was notorious for its abrupt lay-offs.

**Tension between the Hartsteins
continues to mount.**

"It's a new diet dessert. It has 400 calories but the average person will burn 500 calories trying to open the package."

"Congratulations, Mr. Albright! We just found out that you're going to be on the cover of next month's issue of *Bone and Ligament Journal!*"

"There's no need for concern, folks!
This is only a precaution!"

Having lost their list of who each wedding gift
was from, newlyweds Todd and Lori Dretmer
enlisted the help of a psychic.

"Well, let's see. He's positive for hay fever,
negative for mildew, positive for poison ivy,
positive for bee stings, positive for poison sumac.
Let's see how he does with the fire ants."

Chuck's fascination with macrame was
beginning to annoy Coach Paparella.

"Believe it or not, this particular
tooth-extracting device was designed
by a guy who makes corkscrews."

The Mendricks began showcasing their son's talents
long before he was even born.

"This way the kids think twice before they
come charging into the kitchen!"

Having forgotten to save room for his dessert,
Duane switches to his reserve stomach.

Gino's dispute with the neighbors down
in 12-C reaches a climax.

"Hi, Mrs. Franconi! We just stopped by to show you the check you would have received had you returned our envelope that said, 'You Are A Winner!' But since you had better things to do than fill out our silly old prize form . . ."

Another first date is ruined by an embarrassing commercial.

At the Northeastern Dental Academy practice range.

"I volunteered you for a study by the National Sinus Foundation."

"According to the computerized fitness monitor, you died eight and one-half minutes ago."

Al loved to take photos of his customers the instant after they looked at their repair bill.

"I'm sure you'll find today's dissection both challenging and enlightening."

"When Fufu's head droops down and touches his knees, you buzz me!"

"All right, Tom! It's time I ended this charade! I'm not Glenda, your adoring wife of twelve years! I'm IRS agent Lola Schwantz, and I know every tax trick you've tried to pull! Get ready for the mother of all audits!"

In addition to being practical,
PIN tattoos are becoming chic.

"Let's see . . . foot cramps, foot cramps . . . here we go!
It says you should increase your intake of potassium."

The Galsteins were experiencing some serious
communication problems.

**The latest in greeting card technology:
audio birth announcements.**

Ray loved a bargain.

A diabolical new testing technique: math essay questions.

"That new dentist of ours is starting to get on my nerves."

As an expression of his undying love for her,
Dave made Jamie a prom dress in wood shop.

"So you found a chunk of the cat's fur on the floor. Big deal! It's spring! Cat's shed in the spring!"

"We were pretty worried about you until we discovered that the power on the X-ray machine was set way too high and we had actually gotten an image of a coat rack in the room behind you."

"A one-year membership is $10,000, but to encourage you to work out, we give you back $25 every time you use the facility."

HELMET MOUNTED PLUNGER
• GENERATES 5 TIMES THE FORCE OF TRADITIONAL PLUNGERS

"Well, all I know is the man at the hardware store told me it was five times as effective as a standard plunger! Leave it to you to criticize something before you try it!"

"Next I want you to hold your doll with one hand and then lightly rub a piece of beef on the pull tab of the diaper."

"No more emptying the litter box for us! I've trained her to crawl through our heat duct until she reaches the basement of the neighbors in 4-C, where she uses their cat's litter box!"

"Ironically, we were driving across the country because my husband is afraid of flying."

"It not only won't give my card back, it also just sucked my wallet into the deposit slot."

"That monitor can distinguish between real crying and fake crying. If it senses a fake cry, it simply filters it out."

"I swear, all I did was hit the trunk release lever!"

"Since it's almost certain you'll need another bypass
in ten years, we were wondering if we could implant
this small time capsule in you as a gesture of
goodwill to the surgeons who will work on you then."

Having flunked three consecutive chemistry tests, Brad got home one day to discover that his parents had wallpapered his room with the periodic chart.

Before allowing Becky to go on a first date,
Mr. Dortmeyer would review past episodes
of "America's Most Wanted."

"As part of our commitment to customer service,
Dominick will visit you three times a week to
encourage you to use the bike regularly."

After acing five consecutive calculus tests, Duane
was able to land a lucrative endorsement deal.

**Although the wine tasted fine,
Gary had always wanted to do this.**

"Where the heck did you find this stuff?"

A hideous development in air travel:
karaoke flights.

Clepman Industries decided to make an example of anyone who abused the sick-leave system.